IN MEMORY OF JAKE

The Salty Dog Inc.
224 South Sea Pines Drive
Hilton Head Island, South Carolina 29928

Version 2, Second Printing 2005

THE LEGEND OF JAKE, THE SALTY DOG

Written By Robbie Biscayne
Illustrated By Mark Yarbrough

John earned his living as a fisherman.

Jake shared John's love for the sea.

Early one Friday morning,
John powered up their
36-foot fishing vessel
and headed for the deep
blue sea.

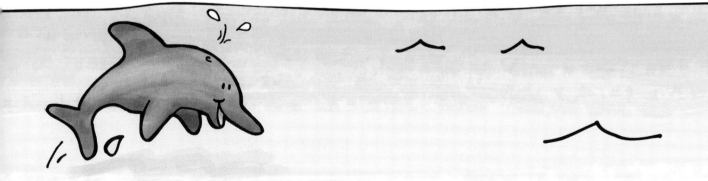

A dolphin jumped so high that he was flying.

Suddenly, the sky began to darken and the wind whipped to 60 knots.

Then out of nowhere, the Salty Dog was slammed by a 20-foot rogue wave.

Jake dug his paws into the deck and tried to fend off the storm with his mightiest growl.

Jake and John were tossed into the raging sea.

Jake instinctively swam to his master's side.

John began to lose hope as he watched their boat sink
to the bottom of the Atlantic Ocean, but...

Jake refused to give up.
He paddled hard and headed
in a westerly direction.

Jake swam for three days...

Jake just kept going until...

... he had paddled all the way back to South Beach.

Jake had *saved* their lives!

Jake's place in nautical history is assured.

Meanwhile, The Wreck of the Salty Dog settled to the bottom of the Atlantic awaiting discovery...